I'm Not Happy

Written by Sue Graves

Illustrated by
Desideria Guicciardini

On Friday, Ben went to play at his friend Amir's house.

Amir had broken his best truck.
"I'm not happy!"
he said.

Ben wanted to help Amir.
He **helped** him to mend his truck.

Amir was very happy.

In the afternoon, Ben went to play **football** with Tim and Lucy.

But Mick took Tim's football.
Tim was **upset.**

Mick felt **bad.**
He gave the ball back to Tim.

They all played football together.
Everyone was **happy!**

Then Ben saw Molly and her mum. Molly was **upset.**

12

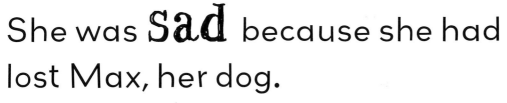

She was **sad** because she had
lost Max, her dog.
"I can't find him anywhere!" she cried.

Ben **felt sorry** for Molly.
He **helped** her look for Max.

They looked in the bushes. But they couldn't find Max **anywhere.**

Just then, Ben's mum came along.
She said Ben had to go to Gran's house.
"You must put on the jumper that Gran
made for you," she told Ben.

But Ben **didn't like** the jumper.
It was too big and too scratchy!
Ben was **not happy.**

17

But Gran was **delighted** to see Ben
in the jumper.

She was so **happy**, it made Ben feel **happy** too!

Ben told Gran about Molly's dog, Max.
He told her that Molly was feeling
miserable. Gran had a good idea.
She helped Ben make some posters.

Then they put up the posters all around the **park**.

That night, there was a knock at Ben's door. It was a man ...

... and he had **Max** with him! The man told Ben he had seen his posters. "Then I saw Max in my street!" he said.

Everyone was **happy...**

...but Max was the
happiest of all!

Can you tell the story of what happens when the boy's balloon flies away?

How do you think he felt when he lost his balloon?

How did he feel at the end?

A note about sharing this book

The *Our Emotions and Behaviour* series has been developed to provide a starting point for further discussion on children's feelings and behaviour, both in relation to themselves and to other people.

I'm Not Happy

This story explores in a reassuring way some of the typical situations that can make people unhappy. It explores how we can help ourselves feel better when we are sad, and how we can make others feel better.

The book aims to encourage children to have a developing awareness of their own needs, views and feelings, and to be sensitive to the needs, views and feelings of others.

Storyboard puzzle

The wordless storyboard on pages 26 and 27 provides an opportunity for speaking and listening. Children are encouraged to tell the story illustrated in the panels: the little boy is sad when he accidentally knocks into the girl and his balloon flies away. He is cheered up when the girl helps him get his balloon back.

How to use the book

The book is designed for adults to share with either an individual child, or a group of children, and as a starting point for discussion.

The book also provides visual support and repeated words and phrases to build confidence in children who are starting to read on their own.

Before reading the story

Choose a time to read when you and the children are relaxed and have time to share the story.

Spend time looking at the illustrations and talk about what the book may be about before reading it together.

28

After reading, talk about the book with the children:

- What was it about? Have the children ever felt unhappy? What made them unhappy? Have they ever broken a favourite toy? Who helped them to feel better and how?

- Talk about Tim and Molly's experiences in the story. Have the children had similar experiences? Encourage the children to take turns to share their experiences with the others and to listen without interrupting.

- Talk about Mick taking Tim's ball away and how this made Tim sad. Do the children think that this made Mick feel happy? How did Mick make Tim feel better? What would they do if they made someone feel unhappy? Talk about the importance of saying "sorry".

- Extend this discussion by talking about other occasions when the children might feel unhappy. Do they feel unhappy when they have to face new situations? Provide possible scenarios, for example, are they shy about making new friends? How did they feel, for example, when they went to school for the first time? Did they know anyone in their class before?

- Spend time talking about strategies for overcoming shyness or loneliness that can lead to unhappiness. Similarly, talk about ways of cheering themselves up. For example, do they have favourite toys that they like to cuddle when they are unhappy?

- Now talk about the things that might make adults unhappy. For example would they, too, be sad if a pet went missing or a friend moved away? What could they do to make themselves feel better?

- Take the opportunity to talk about welcoming new children to school. How could the children help them to settle in so that they feel happy in their new school?

- Look at the storyboard puzzle. Can they draw a picture of what makes them feel better when they are unhappy?

First published in 2011 by
Franklin Watts
338 Euston Road
London
NW1 3BH

Franklin Watts Australia
Level 17/207 Kent Street
Sydney
NSW 2000

A CIP catalogue record for this book is available
from the British Library.

ISBN 978 1 4451 0153 8

Editors: Adrian Cole and Jackie Hamley
Designers: Jonathan Hair and Peter Scoulding

Printed in China

Franklin Watts is a division of
Hachette Children's Books,
an Hachette UK company.
www.hachette.co.uk